WHEN FOOD IS A JOURNEY.
MEXICAN RECIPES.

by Elì Arteaga

Dining with the Mayans

TABLE OF CONTENTS

CHICKEN ENCHILADAS WITH PASILLA CHILI SAUCE	6
CHICKEN FAJITAS	11
CHICKEN IN SPICY BROWN SAUCE	13
CHICKEN OR BEEF FAJITAS	15
CHICKEN SOPAPILLA (INCL. TORTILLAS)	17
CHICKEN TACO CASSEROLE	20
CHICKEN TACOS	22
CHICKEN TEQUILA	24
CHICKEN TORTILLA CASSEROLE	26
CHICKEN WITH AVOCADO SALSA	27
CHILAQUILES (A CASSEROLE OF TORTILLAS IN CHILI)	29
CHILE CON QUESO	32
CHILE PIQUIN SAUCE	33
CHILES RELLENOS (FRIED STUFFED CHILES)	34
CHILES RELLENOS CASSEROLE	36

CHILES RELLENOS CASSEROLE W/MARINARA	38
CHILES RELLENOS CON QUESOS	40
CHILES RELLENOS DE QUESO 2	42
CHILES RELLENOS DE SAN DIEGO	45
CHILES RELLENOS MEATBALLS	47
CHILI BEEF TACOS	49
CHILI POBLANO PIE	52
CHILI RELLENO'S FAST AND EASY	55
CHILIES RELLENOS WITH CHEESE	57
CHIMICHANGAS DE PAPAS	59
CHIMICHANGAS SUPREME PART 1	61
CHIMICHANGAS SUPREME PART 2	63
CHIPOTLE CHILES	65
CHIPOTLE MAYONNAISE	69
CHIPOTLE SAUCE	70
CHORIZO	72

CHURROS DE PLATANO (FRIED PLANTAINS)	74
CILANTRO PESTO	76
CINCO DE MAYO CASSEROLE	77
CITRUS BARBECUE SAUCE	79
CORN AND WALNUT DIP	81
CORN SALSA	82
CORN TORTILLAS	83
CORN-SALSA PITA SANDWICHES	85
COWBOY CAVIAR	88
CROCKPOT CHILE STEW	90
CUCUMBER SALSA	91
DELUXE NACHOS	92
DIABLO JALAPENO JELLY	94
EASY NACHOS	97
EGG TACOS	99
EGGS MOTUL STYLE	101

Copyright 2021 by Elì Arteaga All rights reserved.

In no way is it legal to reproduce, duplicate, or transmit any part of this document in either electronic means or in printed format. Recording of this publication is strictly prohibited, and any storage of this document is not allowed unless with written permission from the publisher. All rights reserved.

The information provided herein is stated to be truthful and consistent, in that any liability, in terms of inattention or otherwise, by any usage or abuse of any policies, processes, or directions contained within is the solitary and utter responsibility of the recipient reader. Under no circumstances will any legal responsibility or blame be held against the publisher for any reparation, damages, or monetary loss due to the information herein, either directly or indirectly. Respective authors own all copyrights not held by the publisher.

Legal Notice:

This book is copyright protected. This is only for personal use. You cannot amend, distribute, sell, use, quote, or paraphrase any part of the content within this book without the consent of the author or copyright owner. Legal action will be pursued if this is breached.

Disclaimer Notice:

Please note the information contained within this document is for educational and entertainment purposes only. Every attempt has been made to provide accurate, up-to-date, and reliable, complete information. No warranties of any kind are expressed or implied. Readers acknowledge that the author is not engaging in the rendering of legal, financial, medical, or professional advice.

By reading this document, the reader agrees that under no circumstances are we responsible for any losses, direct or indirect, which are incurred as a result of the use of the information contained within this document, including, but not limited to, —errors, omissions, or inaccuracies

CHICKEN ENCHILADAS WITH PASILLA CHILI SAUCE

Ingredients

- 2 tablespoons Peanut oil
- 1 2-oz. package dried pasilla
- Chilies stemmed, seeded, torn into 1-inch pieces
- 1/2 cup Whole blanched almonds Chopped
- 4 Chicken breast halves
- 6 cups Chicken stock or canned

- Low-salt broth
- 1/2 teaspoon Cumin seeds
- 4 Plum tomatoes, cored Quartered
- 1/2 onion - quartered
- 4 cloves garlic - peeled
- 2 tablespoons firmly packed golden brown Sugar
- 1 teaspoon Coarse salt
- Peanut oil (for deep frying)
- 16 Corn tortillas
- 2 1/2 cups grated Monterey Jack Cheese
- 1 cup Creme fraiche or sour cream
- 1 Avocado, peeled, seeded, sliced
- Fresh cilantro sprigs

Directions

Heat 2 tablespoons of oil in a large pot over high heat. Add chilies and almonds. Saute until chilies darken and almonds are golden for about 2 minutes. Using a slotted spoon, transfer chilies and almonds to the bowl.

Reduce heat to medium. Season chicken with salt and pepper. Add to the same pot and brown on all sides, about 5 minutes. Add stock; simmer until chicken is cooked through, about 20 minutes. Transfer chicken to another bowl using a slotted spoon; cool. Reserve stock in a pot.

Toast cumin seeds in a heavy small skillet over medium-low heat until aromatic, about 1 minute. Mince cumin seeds. Add cumin, chili mixture, tomatoes, quartered onion, garlic, sugar, and salt to stock. Simmer until all ingredients are very soft, about 45 minutes.

Working in batches, puree stock mixture in a blender. Return to pot. Boil until reduced to 4 cups, occasionally stirring, about 20 minutes. Season with salt and pepper. (Can be made 1 day ahead. Chill chicken and sauce separately.)

Remove skin from chicken and discard. Cut meat from bones and shred.

Transfer to a bowl and combine with 1/2 cup sauce. Set filling aside.

Oil two 13X9-inch glass baking dishes. Pour oil into a deep skillet to a depth of 1/2 inch and heat to 375-degree F. Fry tortillas 1 at a time until softened, about 5 seconds per side. Using a metal spatula, transfer to paper towels. Spread 1 tablespoon sauce over each tortilla. Sprinkle each with 2 tablespoons cheese and 1 tablespoon chopped onion. Place 1/3 cup chicken down the center of each tortilla; roll-up. Place seam side down in baking dishes. (Can be made 1 hour ahead. Cover.)

Preheat oven to 350-degree F. Pours remaining sauce over enchiladas.

Sprinkle with remaining cheese. Bake until heated through, about 20 minutes. Top with creme fraiche, avodado and clinatro.

CHICKEN FAJITAS

Ingredients

- 6" Flour Tortillas
- Sm Onion - sliced into rings
- Cloves Garlic - minced
- Med Green /Sweet Red Pepper*
- 1 tablespoon Cooking Oil
- 9 ounces Chicken Breast halves **
- 1/3 cup Salsa
- 2 cups Shredded Lettuce

- 1/4 cup Plain low-fat Yogurt
- Green onion - thinly sliced

* Cut into bite-size strips ** 9 oz boned skinless chicken breast halves, cut into bite-sized strips

Directions

Wrap tortillas in foil. Place in 300deg F. oven for 10-12 minutes or till heated through. Meanwhile, spray a large skillet with Pam. Add onion and garlic; stir-fry for 2 minutes. Add red or green pepper; stir-fry for 1-2 minutes more or until veggies are tender-crisp. Remove from skillet. Add oil to the skillet.

Add chicken; stir-fry 3-5 minutes or till chicken is tender and no longer pink. Return veggies to skillet. Add salsa. Cook and stir till heated through.

To serve, divide the chicken mixture evenly among tortillas. Top with shredded lettuce. Dollop with yogurt and sprinkle with green onion.

Roll up tortillas and serve.

CHICKEN IN SPICY BROWN SAUCE

Ingredients

- 3 Whole chicken breasts – split and skinned
- 2 tablespoons Vegetable oil
- 1 15 oz can tomato sauce
- 1/2 cup Picante sauce
- 4 teaspoons unsweetened cocoa powder
- 1 teaspoon ground cumin
- 1 teaspoon Oregano
- 1/2 teaspoon Garlic salt

Directions

Dash EACH: cloves, nutmeg, ground allspice

Pound chicken to 1/2" thick. Lightly brown in oil in a large skillet, about 2 minutes on each side; drain off fat. Combine remaining ingredients; mix well. Pour over chicken in skillet. Bring to boil. Reduce heat; cover and simmer gently,10 minutes. Remove chicken to serving platter; keep warm. Cook and stir sauce until slightly thickened, about 3 to 5 minutes. Spoon sauce over chicken.

Makes 6 servings.

CHICKEN OR BEEF FAJITAS

Ingredients

- 1/2 cup Vegetable oil
- 1/2 cup Lime juice
- 1 cup Tequila
- 1/4 cup Tomato paste
- 2 Garlic cloves - minced
- 1 Whole jalapeno pepper
- 1/2 teaspoon salt
- 1/2 teaspoon Chili powder
- 1/2 teaspoon Cumin
- 1 1/2 pounds Chicken breast*
- 10 Flour tortillas for fajitas
- 3 tablespoons Vegetable oil
- 1 large bell pepper - cut into
- 1 large onion - cut into strips
- 1 large tomato - cut into chunks

*Boneless, skinless breast, cut into strips; or skirt steak.

Directions

In a glass bowl or baking dish, combine 1/2 cup oil, lime juice, tequila, tomato paste, garlic, jalapeno, salt, chili powder, and cumin. Blend well.

Add the chicken, cover, and marinate in the refrigerator for at least 6 hours or overnight. Wrap tortillas in aluminum foil. Bake 15 minutes while preparing fajitas. Remove chicken from marinade.

In a large, heavy skillet over medium-high heat, heat 3 Tbl oil, add chicken, and cook, stirring constantly, 5 to 7 minutes or until chicken is done. Add bell pepper and onion and cook 3 minutes more along with tomatoes, just until vegetables are crisp-tender. Serve with tortillas, guacamole, sour cream, salsa, and grated cheese.

CHICKEN SOPAPILLA (INCL. TORTILLAS)

Ingredients

- 2 cups all-purpose flour
- 1/2 teaspoon salt
- 2 teaspoons baking powder
- 1 tablespoon shortening - (lard is best)
- 3/4 cup warm water
- oil for deep frying
- cooked, cut up, or shredded chicken
- salsa

Directions

Mix the flour, salt, and baking powder together. Cut in the shortening. Mix until it resembles cornmeal.

Stir in the water until all the dough is moist.

Turn onto a floured surface and knead for about 5 minutes. Cover with plastic wrap or towel and let rest for 30 minutes.

Cut the batch in half and roll out about 1/4" thick. (These are thicker than ordinary flour tortillas).

Cut into 4 to 5" squares or rounds. (I like around, so use a coffee can to cut)

Heat oil in a deep fryer or skillet to 400 degrees. (I just use a deep iron skillet with about 3" of oil.) and drop, *one at a time in the hot oil until puffed and golden brown (If they don't puff up, the oil's not hot enough)

Take out of the skillet and lay on paper towels. Continue until you have as many as you want. Let cool a little.

Take chicken or pork and mix with salsa. Heat chicken in salsa over the stove before you stuff.

Carefully slit one side of the Sopapilla and put in about 3 tablespoons of the chicken.

Serve on a platter with each Sopapilla on a leaf of Romaine Lettuce and Salsa Fresca on the side to put over/or in them. This is a last-minute, labor-intensive procedure, but they are simply wonderful.

CHICKEN TACO CASSEROLE

Ingredients

- 1 large Chopped onion
- 3 tablespoons Margarine
- 1 can Chopped chilies (small)
- 2 cups Tomato juice
- 1 can Cheddar cheese soup
- 1 teaspoon Chili powder
- 1/4 teaspoon Garlic powder

- 2 cups Chopped chicken breast - cooked
- 1 Dozen tortillas
- 1 cup Grated cheese

Directions

Saute onion in butter. Add chilies, tomato juice, cheddar cheese soup, chili powder, and garlic powder. Add chopped chicken. Break tortillas into about 6 pieces each. Put a layer of tortillas, a layer of chicken mixture, and a layer of grated cheese. Repeat until all is used. Bake at 350 degrees for about 30 minutes in a 2-quart casserole, covered, and then uncover and add more grated cheese and cook until cheese is melted. This serves about 8.

CHICKEN TACOS

Ingredients

- 1/4 cup Green onion - chopped
- 1 tablespoon Shortening
- 2 cups cooked chicken - shredded
- 1 each 8 oz can taco sauce or 8 ounces Green chili salsa
- 1 each Salt to taste
- 1 package taco shells
- 1 cup grated cheddar cheese

-OPTIONAL TOPPINGS-

- 1 each Chopped lettuce
- 1 each Chopped tomato
- 1 each Sour cream
- 1 each Guacamole

Directions

Saute' the onion in the shortening until transparent. Add the chicken, green chili salsa, or taco sauce and salt to taste. Heat to boiling.

Prepare shells according to package directions. Put two tablespoons of the chicken mixture and one tablespoon of grated cheese in each shell. Serve with the option of lettuce, tomato, sour cream, or guacamole and extra chili sauce as desired.

CHICKEN TEQUILA

Ingredients

- 1 cup Strong chicken stock
- 9 ounces Whole tomatoes - undrained
- 3 cloves garlic - minced
- 2 Chicken breasts - boneless
- 1/2 cup Tequila
- 2 Juice from two limes
- Heavy dash cayenne pepper
- 1 teaspoon Chili powder

- 1 teaspoon Cumin
- 1/2 teaspoon Coriander
- Salt to taste
- Olive oil

Directions

Simmer the chicken breasts in the stock until tender. Remove and cube.

Set aside, reserving stock. Saute' the garlic in olive oil. Add tomatoes (breaking up) and the remaining ingredients; simmer, covered 1/2 hour. Add chicken and re-heat. Toss with cooked noodles. If the sauce becomes too thick, add the chicken stock. Sprinkle with Parmesan cheese and garnish with fresh basil or parsley leaves.

CHICKEN TORTILLA CASSEROLE

Ingredients

- 6 Corn tortillas
- 1/2 cup Milk
- 1/2-pound Cheddar cheese - shredded
- 1 can green chili salsa
- 1 can Cream of mushroom soup
- 1 can Cream of chicken soup
- 3 Chicken breasts; cooked - cut up

Directions

Cut or tear the tortillas in 1/2" squares. Put half of them on the bottom of a baking dish and cover with 1/2 of the cheese. Mix salsa, both soups, and chicken together. Add half of this mixture to the baking dish. Repeat the layers and top with cheese. Cover and put in the fridge for 24 hours. Bake at 350~F for 45 min. Uncover for the last 15 minutes to brown.

CHICKEN WITH AVOCADO SALSA

Ingredients

- 1-pound boneless chicken breast - halves
- Chili powder - salt and pepper
- 1 Ripe avocado
- 1 tablespoon fresh lime juice
- 1/2 cup Chunky salsa
- 1 Tomato - chopped
- 2 Green onions with - tops, thinly sliced
- 4 Heated corn tortillas or - lettuce leaves

Directions

Arrange chicken around the edges of a 9" pie plate or baking dish.

Sprinkle with chili powder, salt, and pepper. Cover with vented plastic wrap.

Rotating dish midway through cooking, microwave on high 5 to 6 minutes; set aside. Peel, seed, and chop avocado. Combine with lime juice in a small bowl. Add salsa, tomato, and green onions; toss gently. Slice cooked chicken, lengthwise, into 1 to 2" strips and arrange on tortillas, making 4 servings. Top with salsa. Microwave on 50 % (medium) for 2 minutes or until heated.

Makes 4 servings.

CHILAQUILES (A CASSEROLE OF TORTILLAS IN CHILI)

Ingredients

- 1/2-pound Queso fresco, crumbled – or mild Cheddar – grated 1-1/3 cups
- 18 Stale tortillas - cut into or triangles
- 1 cup Thin sour cream
- 2 Chorizos - crumbled and 1 medium Onion - thinly sliced into

- 2 limes - cut into wedges
- Ready: A flameproof dish at 3 Inches deep and about 10 inches across

Directions

THE SAUCE

Heat the griddle and toast the chilies lightly on both sides. Be careful- they burn very quickly. When they are cool enough to handle, remove the seeds and veins. Cover the chiles with hot water to cover and leave them to soak for about 20 minutes, then transfer with a slotted spoon to the blender jar. Add the rest of the ingredients and blend them into a smooth sauce.

THE CHILAQUILES:

In a small frying pan, add 2 Tbsp. peanut or safflower oil, 1/2 cup chicken broth. Heat the oil and cook the sauce until it darkens in color and is well seasoned-about 3 minutes. Add the broth and let the sauce cook over a high flame for a few minutes longer. Set aside.

Heat the oil and fry the tortilla strips until they are pale gold but not too crisp. Remove and drain on the toweling.

Cover the bottom of the dish with one-third of the tortilla pieces. Cover them with a layer of one-third of the cheese and a layer of one-third of the sauce. Repeat the layers twice more.

Add the 3 to 3-1/2 cups chicken broth and bring to a boil. Lower the flame and continue cooking the chilaquiles at a brisk simmer until most of the broth has been absorbed - about 15 minutes. Add the epazote a minute or so before the chilaquiles have finished cooking. (2 large sprigs.)

Pour the sour cream around the edge of the dish, then garnish with the chorizos and the onion rings. Serve in small deep bowls with lime wedges on the side.

CHILE CON QUESO

Ingredients

- 1 cup Cheese - Shredded *
- 4 ounces Green Chiles**
- 1/4 cup Half & Half
- 2 tablespoons Onion - Finely Chopped
- 2 teaspoons Cumin - Ground
- 1/2 teaspoon salt

*Use either Cheddar or Monterey Jack Cheese (4 oz).

**Use 1 4-oz can of chopped green chiles, drained.

Directions

Heat all ingredients over low heat, constantly stirring, until the cheese is melted.

Serve warm with tortilla chips. Makes 1 1/4 cups dip.

CHILE PIQUIN SAUCE

- 1-ounce Dried chile Piquin
- 1/4 teaspoon Cumin
- 1/4 cup Oil
- 8 ounces Tomato sauce
- 1/2 teaspoon Chopped fresh garlic

Directions

Heat oil until hot and remove from heat, pour chile into frying for about 2 min in hot oil, then drain on paper towels. Put chile, tomato sauce, cumin, and garlic in blender and mix add salt to your taste

CHILES RELLENOS (FRIED STUFFED CHILES)

Ingredients

- 12 larges Mild - green chiles w/stems or 3 cans green chiles (4 oz. CNS)
- 1/2-pound Jack cheese cut into long narrow - strips.

-BATTER-

- 1 cup all-purpose flour
- 1 teaspoon Baking powder
- 1/2 teaspoon salt
- 3/4 cup yellow or white cornmeal
- 1 cup Milk
- 2 eggs - slightly beaten

Directions

Parch and peel chiles leaving stems on. Cut small slit below the stem, removing seeds if desired.

Insert strips of Jack cheese, being careful not to split chile.

Prepare the batter: Sift flour with baking powder and salt, then add cornmeal. Blend milk and slightly beaten eggs, then combine the milk mixture with the dry mixture and blend together. Slightly moisten each chile with water-dip in plain flour, then in batter. Allow to drain slightly and drop in deep fat, which has been heated to 375 F.

Fry until golden. Drain on paper towels. Keep warm on a platter at 300 F.

oven while completing frying and serve immediately.

Variations: For a thicker crust, "double-dip" (repeat dipping sequence).

For the crunchy crust, use buttermilk instead of sweet milk in the batter.

Hint: Keep one hand for "dry," the other for "wet."

CHILES RELLENOS CASSEROLE

Ingredients

- 2 cans Whole green chili peppers*
- 3 cups Sharp Cheddar cheese**
- 4 each Green onions - sliced
- 3 cups shredded mozzarella cheese
- 6 each Egg
- 4 cups Milk
- 3/4 cup all-purpose flour
- 1/4 teaspoon salt
- 2 cans green chili salsa

* 7 oz. cans **shredded (approx. 12 oz.) Split chili peppers lengthwise and remove seeds and pith.

Directions

Spread chilies in a single layer in a greased 9x13-inch baking dish. Sprinkle Cheddar cheese, green onions, and 1-1/2 cups of mozzarella cheese over chilies. In a bowl, beat eggs, milk, flour, and salt together until smooth. Pour over chilies and cheese. Bake in a 325 degrees oven for 50 minutes or until a knife inserted in the custard comes out clean.

Meanwhile, mix salsa with the remaining 1-1/2 cups mozzarella cheese.

Sprinkle over casserole and return to oven for 10 minutes or until cheese melts. Let stand for 5 minutes before serving.

CHILES RELLENOS CASSEROLE W/MARINARA

Ingredients

- 4 pounds Jack cheese - cut in strips
- 1 can 4 oz green chiles - seeded
- 4 Eggs
- 1/3 cup Milk
- 1/2 cup Flour
- 1/2 teaspoon Baking powder

- 1 cup grated sharp cheddar cheese
- 1 can Marinara sauce
- Pitted ripe olives(garnish)

Directions

Stuff chilies w/jack cheese. Arrange chilies side-by-side in greased shallow 1 1/2 qt. baking dish.

Beat eggs until thick and foamy; add milk, flour, and baking powder - blend.

Pour egg batter over chiles - cover all chiles with batter. Sprinkle with cheddar cheese. Bake uncovered 375 for 30 minutes or until set. Serve with heated marinara sauce and olives.

CHILES RELLENOS CON QUESOS

Ingredients

- 8 Fresh - frozen or 2 (4 oz) green chilies
- 1 pound Monterey jack cheese
- 4 Eggs
- 4 tablespoons butter - margarine or lard (garnish)

Directions

Peel fresh peppers by placing them on an open flame until browned. Wrap chilies in a damp cloth to steam for five minutes. Pull peeling off.

Slit green chiles. Cut cheese into slices that will fit into the green chile slits. (Be sure to remove seeds and membrane) Prepare a batter by using one egg for every two chiles and one tsp of hot water for each egg, plus enough flour (1 tbsp per egg) to make a thin batter. Beat egg whites until they form soft peaks. Fold in beaten egg yolks and flour.

Drop the batter (the size of a 6-in.x4-in. oval) onto a greased frypan. Place a stuffed chile on it and cover with batter. Cook over low heat until golden. Turn with spatula and brown on the other side. Drain on paper towels. Place in a baking dish, cover with sauce, and top with grated cheese.

Heat in 325 F oven until cheese melts (about 15 mins)

CHILES RELLENOS DE QUESO 2

Ingredients

- 2 Chiles, calif. - roast & peel
- 1 1/3 ounces Cheese - Monterey jack
- Oil - for frying
- 1 egg - separated
- 1/8 cup flour - all-purpose

TOMATO SAUCE

- 1 1/3 small Tomatoes - peeled
- 1/3 small Onion
- 1/3 Garlic clove
- 1/3 tablespoon Oil - vegetable
- 1/8 cup Chicken broth
- 1/8 teaspoon salt
- 2/3 small Chiles - calif.
- Cinnamon, ground
- Cloves, ground

Directions

Prepare tomato sauce; keep warm.

Cut as small a slit as possible in one side of each chile to remove

seeds. Leave stems on. Pat chiles dry with paper towels.

Cut cheese into long thin sticks, one for each chile. Place one stick in each chile, using more if chiles are large. If chiles are loose and open, wrap around cheese and fasten with wooden picks.

Pour oil 1/4" deep into a large skillet. Heat oil to 365° F. Beats egg whites in a medium bowl until stiff. Beat egg yolks lightly in a small bowl and add all at once to beaten egg whites.

Fold lightly but thoroughly. Roll chiles in flour, then dip in egg mixture to coat.

Fry in hot oil until golden brown, turning with a spatula. Drain on paper towels. Serve immediately topped with tomato sauce.

Tomato Sauce: Combine tomatoes, onion, and garlic in blender or food processor; puree. Heat oil in a medium saucepan, add the tomato mixture. Cook 10 minutes, stirring occasionally. Add broth, salt, chiles, cloves, and cinnamon. Simmer gently for 15 minutes.

CHILES RELLENOS DE SAN DIEGO

Ingredients

- 1 package taco seasoning mix
- 16 ounces tomatoes
- 7 ounces green chiles - canned
- 1/4-pound Monterey jack cheese - *see note
- salt - optional
- 1/4 cup flour
- 2 eggs
- 1/4 teaspoon cream of tartar
- 1 cup Canola oil

*Cut the cheese into 6 strips.

Directions

For the spicy tomato sauce, which goes on top, combine the taco seasoning mix and tomatoes in a saucepan. Bring to a boil, reduce heat and simmer for 15 minutes.

If fresh chiles are used, cut off the stem ends and rinse with cold water to remove seeds. Broil the chiles until the skin browns and blisters. Peel the chiles immediately while they are still warm. If canned chiles are used, gently rinse with cold water to remove seeds; pat dry. Stuff each chile with a strip of cheese.

Combine the flour and salt.

Separate the eggs. Beat yolks until lemon yellow and slightly thickened. Beat the whites until they are foamy. Add the cream of tartar and continue beating until the whites hold a stiff peak. Carefully fold yolks into whites.

Heat the oil in a skillet.

Roll the stuffed chiles in the flour. Dip into the egg batter. Fry in hot oil on each side until golden. Drain and serve with spicy tomato sauce.

Yield: 6 Rellenos.

CHILES RELLENOS MEATBALLS

Ingredients

- 12 small potatoes, or 2 large baking potatoes
- 2 tablespoons vegetable oil
- 1 pound ground beef
- 1/2-pound Anaheim chili peppers
- 1/2 cup yellow onions - minced
- 4 eggs
- 1/2 teaspoon salt
- black pepper - to taste
- garlic salt - to taste

*Anaheim chilies, roasted, peeled, and diced.

Directions

Peel and boil potatoes until just tender. Let potatoes cool. In a large bowl, break up potatoes to make a lumpy mixture, do not mash.

Saute ground beef in 2 tablespoons vegetable oil until browned; drain well.

Add beef to potatoes, then add chiles, chopped onion, and egg yolks. Add seasonings (salt, pepper, and garlic salt). Mix and form into egg-shaped balls about 1-1/2 inches long.

Dip each ball in egg whites (beaten slightly), then roll in flour. At medium heat, cook in vegetable oil about 1/4-inch deep. Brown well, then drain on paper towels. Serve hot, at room temperature, or refrigerate and reheat at serving time.

CHILI BEEF TACOS

Ingredients

- 1/4 cup Chili powder
- 6 Garlic cloves - crushed
- 5 tablespoons Strained fresh lime juice
- 3 tablespoons Olive oil
- 1 tablespoon Cumin
- 2 1/2 pounds Stewing beef cut into 1/2 in
- 28 ounces Italian plum tomatoes Drained and crushed
- 2 cups Beef broth
- 12 ounces bottle dark beer
- 1 Large onion chopped
- 2 Jalapeno chilies - minced
- 10 ounces Pkg. frozen corn - thawed and
- 25 Pimento stuffed green olives
- 1/2 cup Pimentos - drained chopped
- Salt and pepper
- 20 Taco shells
- 12 ounces sharp cheddar cheese - shredded

- 1/2 Bunch romaine lettuce - chopped
- 4 Chopped seeded tomatoes
- Hot or mild salsa
- 1 cup Sour cream

Directions

Mix chili powder, garlic, lime juice, 3 Tbs. Olive oil and cumin in a large bowl to form a paste. Add the beef and mix till coated. Refrigerate for 24 hours, stirring occasionally. Position rack in the lower third of the oven and preheat to 350 F. Combine marinated beef, canned tomatoes, broth, and beer in a Dutch oven.

Bring to boil over high heat. Cover, transfer to the oven, and bake for 45 mins. Uncover and continue baking until beef is tender, about 45 minutes more. Cool, shred beef, and return to cooking liquid. Cover and refrigerate overnight.

Heat 3 Tbs. oil in a heavy skillet over medium-low heat.

Add onion and jalapenos, then cover and cook until onion is tender and lightly browned, occasionally stirring, about 15 mins. Strain beef cooking liquid into skillet; bring to a boil. Reduce heat and simmer uncovered until sauce is thickened and reduced to 1/2 cup, occasionally stirring about 50 mins.

Mix in beef. (Can be prepared 1 day in advance and refrigerated). Add corn, olives, and pimentos and stir over medium heat until just heated through about 5 minutes. Season with salt and pepper to taste.

To assemble Half-fill taco shells with beef mixture.

Top with cheese, lettuce, and chopped tomatoes. Serve immediately, passing salsa and sour cream separately.

Note: The same filling also works in chimichangas and enchiladas and is deliciously spooned over toasted hamburger rolls. It can also be frozen.

CHILI POBLANO PIE

Ingredients

- 12 each Poblano chilies - large fresh
- Chihuahua cheese - cubed
- 1 each Garlic clove, large-halved
- 3/4 teaspoon salt
- 1 1/2 cups Whipping cream
- 1/2 pound Monterey jack
- 6 each egg
- 3 tablespoons Sour cream

Directions

Make the Crema Fresca ahead of time: mix Cream and Sour Cream together. Cover and let stand at room temp. Until thickened, 8 hours or overnight. Chill until ready to use. Char the Chili Peppers over a gas flame until blackened on all sides. Wrap them in a plastic bag and let stand for 10 minutes to steam. Peel and core the Chilies.

Remove seeds, rinse and pat dry. Preheat oven to 350 F. Generously Butter a 9" pie pan (preferably porcelain or stoneware with 2" sides).

Open up Chili Peppers and arrange around sides of pan skin side down, point toward the center of the pan, extending about 1/2" above the rim.

Cover the bottom of the pan with Chilies. Finely grate cheese with onion and garlic in a processor using on/off pulses, about 30 seconds. Add Eggs and Salt. Process until smooth, stopping to scrape down the sides, about 15 seconds.

Mix in the Crema Fresca (the Mexican equivalent of creme fraiche). Pour this filling over the Chilies. Curl the edges of the Chilies over the filling. Bake until golden brown and a knife inserted in the center comes out clean, 45 to 50 minutes.

Cover Chili edges with Foil to prevent burning, if necessary.

Cool for 5 minutes before cutting. Serve hot or at room temperature.

CHILI RELLENO'S FAST AND EASY

Ingredients

- 4 large fresh pasilla chilis
- 3 cups grated cheese - used Cheddar
- SAUCE
- 1 sm. can tomato sauce – or 5 fresh tomatoes - chopped
- 1 cup finely chopped scallions - (green onions)
- 1 large clove garlic - finely chopped
- 1 1/2 cups fines chopped fresh cilantro
- 2 teaspoons Charlie's seasoning - heaping
- 3 eggs
- flour - to dip

Directions

I found out you don't have to peel pasilla chilis! Just put them into boiling water for about15 min. Take out, slit open one side, take out the seeds. Don't bother about the membranes; they are not that hot. Rinse under cold water and set aside. (no need to peel)

In a skillet, saute the onions and garlic until almost brown. Add the cilantro, chopped tomatoes or canned tomato sauce, and Charlie's seasoning.

Cook on med. heat until flavors is blended. Set aside.

Grate the cheese and stuff it into the chilis.

Beat the egg white until stiff; add the yolks to the whites, fold in with about 5 tablespoons of flour.

Holding the chilis together, dip into the batter, and then place chilis into a skillet with about a full quarter-inch of hot oil.

You don't need the oil deep. Turn down the stove a little and brown on both sides. Cook until browned and lay the chilis over the heated sauce.

Serve with sliced avocados over the chilis. Mexican cheese sprinkled over the top and sliced radishes.

CHILIES RELLENOS WITH CHEESE

Ingredients

- 6 Poblano chilies
- 1 cup Monterey Jack cheese - cubed
- 1/2 cup Flour
- 3 Eggs
- 1 tablespoon Water
- 1/4 teaspoon salt
- 2 cups Lard or vegetable oil for frying (more if needed)

Directions

Toast chilies on a hot griddle on all sides until skins begin to blister. Place in a plastic bag, seal bag, and allow chilies to steam for 20 minutes.

Peel chilies, and discard skins. Slit chilies lengthwise 1/4 inch from stem to 1/4 inch from the tip.

Remove seeds and piths; leave the stem intact.

Place equal amounts of cheese in chilies. Roll stuffed chilies in flour. Set aside.

Separate eggs; beat whites until stiff. Beat yolks with water and salt; fold into whites. Heat lard or oil in a skillet over medium heat. Dip chilies into the egg mixture. Fry until light golden brown. Drain.

CHIMICHANGAS DE PAPAS

Ingredients

- 1 lb potatoes, mashed - coarsely (4 large)
- 5 oz queso fresco
- 2/3 cup sour cream
- 5 green onions - sliced
- 1 or 2 jalapeno peppers, roasted - peel, seed & chop
- salt and pepper to taste

- flour tortillas
- oil to fry sour cream, green onions, black olives, - and salsa to garnish

Directions

Mix coarsely mashed potatoes, cheese, sour cream, green onions, jalapenos to taste, and salt and pepper to taste.

Fill tortillas fold into a package. Fry in hot oil (one inch in a skillet.) Drain, garnish and serve hot.

This can be the main course or made small and served as an appetizer or a side dish.

This dish can also be made with corn tortillas and baked in an enchilada sauce inside of frying.

CHIMICHANGAS SUPREME PART 1

Ingredients

- 1-pound Lean beef
- 1 teaspoon salt
- 1/4 teaspoon Pepper
- 1/4 teaspoon Garlic powder
- 4 Tomatoes
- 1 1/2 teaspoons Shortening
- 1/2 onion - chopped
- 1/2 Bell pepper - chopped
- 1 1/2 teaspoons Flour
- 1/2 cup canned whole green chiles
- 4 fluid ounces Tortillas
- Oil for deep frying
- Red chile sauce (see index)

Directions

Cut the beef into 4 pieces. Place in a 5 to 6-quart pan and add water to cover. Bring to a boil; skim the foam from the surface. Add the salt, pepper, and garlic. Simmer until tender, approximately 1-1/2 to 2 hours.

Drain the beef, reserving 1/2 cup of the broth.

When the meat is cool, shred. Chop 2 of the tomatoes.

Melt the shortening in a pan over medium heat. Add the onion and bell pepper and saute until tender. Add the flour, whisking until no lumps remain, and cook for 2 minutes. Add the shredded beef, reserved broth, chopped tomatoes, and whole chiles. Simmer 15 minutes.

Place about 1/2 cup of the meat mixture in a line down the center of each tortilla. Fold both ends over 1 inch to 2 inches; fold one side over the other and roll up in a neat package. Secure with a toothpick.

Deep fry in very hot oil (400F) until (See Part 2 for more)

CHIMICHANGAS SUPREME PART 2

(cont. from part 1)

Ingredients

- 1 cup Shredded Wisconsin
- Cheddar cheese
- 1 cup Sour cream
- 4 Black olives
- 1/4 cup Chopped green onions
- 1 tablespoon Whipping cream
- Guacamole (see index)
- 2 cups shredded lettuce
- 4 Black olives

Directions

Crisp and well browned. Drain on paper toweling.

Preheat the broiler. Place the chimichangas on an ovenproof platter or in a baking pan. Spoon Red Chile Sauce over liberally. Sprinkle with grated cheese and green onion. Place under broiler until the cheese melts.

Combine the sour cream and whipping cream. Slice the remaining 2 tomatoes. Top the chimichangas with the sour cream mixture and Guacamole. Garnish with shredded lettuce, sliced tomato, and olives.

CHIPOTLE CHILES

Ingredients

- 1-pound ripe jalapenos

Americans who love the smoky taste and fiery bite of chipotles have recently been hit with high prices and a scarcity of the product. With prices for these smoked jalapenos reaching $15 a pound wholesale, home growers yearn to smoke their own. But the Mexicans have been fairly secretive about their techniques, and none of the books on chiles describe home smoking. After a trip to Delicious Mexico, I think I have solved this mystery - but the process takes some dedication. First, let's look at how the Mexicans do it.

They use a large pot with a rack to smoke-dry the jalapenos. The pit containing the source of heat is underground, with a tunnel leading to the rack. The pods are placed on top of the rack, where drafts of air pull the smoke up and over the pods. The jalapenos can be whole pods or pods without seeds.

The latter are more expensive and are called "Capone's," or castrated ones.

It is possible to make chipotle in the backyard with a meat smoker or

Weber-type barbecue with a lid. The grill should be washed to remove any meat particles because any odor in the barbecue will give the chile an undesirable flavor. Ideally, the smoker or barbecue should be new and dedicated only to smoking chiles.

The quality of homemade chipotle will depend on the maturity and quality of the pods, the moisture in the pods, the temperature of the smoke drying the pods, and the amount of time the peppers are exposed to the smoke and heat. The aroma of wood smoke will flavor the jalapenos, so carefully choose what is burned. Branches from fruit trees, or other hardwoods such as hickory, oak, and pecan, work superbly. Pecan is used extensively in parts of Mexico and in southern New Mexico to flavor chipotle. Do not be afraid to experiment with different woods.

The difference between the fresh weight of the fruits and the finished

product is about ten to one, so it takes ten pounds of fresh jalapenos to produce approximately one pound of chipotles. A pound of chipotles goes a long way, as a single pod is usually enough to flavor a dish.

First, wash all the pods and discard any that have insect damage, bruises, or are soft. Remove the stems from the pods before placing the peppers in a single layer on the grill rack. Start two small fires on each side of the grill with charcoal briquets. Keep the fires small and never directly expose the pods to the fire so they won't dry unevenly or burn. The intention is to dry the pods slowly while flavoring them with smoke. Soak the wood in water before placing it on the coals so the wood will burn slower and create more smoke. The barbecue vents should be opened only partially to allow a small amount of air to enter the barbecue, thus preventing the fires from burning too fast and creating too much heat.

Check the pods and the fires hourly and move the pods around, always keeping them away from the fires. It may take up to forty-eight hours to dry the pods completely. The pods will be hard, light in weight, and brown in color when dried. If necessary, let the fires burn through the night. After the pods have dried, remove them from the grill and let them cool. To preserve their flavor, place them in a zip-lock bag. It is best to store them in a cool and dry location. If humidity is kept out of the bags, the chipotles will last for twelve to twenty-four months.

Buen apetito!

CHIPOTLE MAYONNAISE

Ingredients

- 1/2 cup Mayonnaise
- 1/2 cup Dairy Sour Cream
- 1/8 teaspoon Oregano Leaves; Dried - (Opt.)
- 2 each Chipotle Chiles*

* Chipotle Chiles should be the ones that are canned in adobo sauce and should be finely chopped.

Directions

Mix all ingredients. Cover and refrigerate until chilled, about 1 hour. Makes about 1 cup of mayonnaise

CHIPOTLE SAUCE

Ingredients

- 2 each Chipotle Chiles*
- 2 each Bacon; Slices - Finely Cut Up
- 1/4 cup Onion; Finely Chopped
- 3 cups Tomatoes - Finely Chopped
- 1 cup Beef Broth
- 1/4 cup Carrot - Finely Chopped
- 1/4 cup Celery - Finely Chopped
- 1/4 cup Fresh Cilantro - Snipped
- 1/2 teaspoon salt
- 1/4 teaspoon Pepper

* You can make this sauce as hot as you want by adding up to a total of 4 dried Chipotle chiles.

Directions

Cover chilies with warm water. Let stand until softened, about 1 hour. Drain and finely chop. Cook and stir bacon and onion in a 2-quart saucepan until bacon is crisp; stir in chilies and remaining ingredients. Makes about 4 cups of sauce.

CHORIZO

Ingredients

- 2 pounds Ground beef
- 2 pounds ground pork
- 3 tablespoons Salt
- 2 tablespoons Oregano
- 2 teaspoons Pepper
- 3 teaspoons Garlic
- 1 3/4 cups Vinegar
- 2 cups Chile Powder
- 2 teaspoons Cumin seed

Directions

A very greasy Mexican sausage. This is a leaner version that is good with scrambled eggs, tortillas, and salsa to create Huevos Rancheros.

Pour some water in chile powder and mix to make a paste; add garlic.

Crush oregano and cumin seed together. Combine meats in a large bowl and add the oregano-cumin seed mixture, salt, and pepper, mixing well.

Add the vinegar and mix. Add chili-garlic mixture and mix well. I have not made this, but my husband has, and it is very good. I doubt that the method of putting it together is very critical as long as you get it mixed well. When you have it mixed well, fry a small patty of it to see if it is what you want, and then you can correct the seasonings to your own taste so far as garlic, chile, and such.

CHURROS DE PLATANO (FRIED PLANTAINS)

Ingredients

- 3 plantains - peeled, * see note
- lemon juice
- 4 eggs
- 1/4 cup flour
- 1/2 teaspoon salt
- oil - ** see note

* If plantains (fat, red-skinned cooking bananas) are not available, use large, green-tipped bananas. DO NOT use overripe bananas.

** For frying, use part olive oil, part Canola oil.

Directions

Peel and split the bananas lengthwise. Cut each piece in half and dip in lemon juice.

To make the batter, beat the egg yolks until thick and light. Add flour and salt. Beat egg whites until stiff, not dry, and fold into yolks.

Drop the drained banana pieces into the batter, one at a time. Pick up with a slotted spoon and slide gently into hot oil in a heavy skillet (oil about 1 inch deep). Cook over medium heat, turning almost immediately. Cook until browned on both sides. Drain on paper toweling.

Serving Ideas: Served with meat and poultry in Mexico.

CILANTRO PESTO

Ingredients

- 1 1/2 cups Fresh Cilantro - Firm Packed
- 1/2 cup Parsley - Firmly Packed
- 1/2 cup Parmesan Cheese
- 1/2 cup Vegetable Oil
- 1/4 teaspoon salt
- 3 each Cloves Garlic
- 1/4 cup Pine Nuts - 1 oz

Directions

Place all ingredients in a food processor work bowl fitted with a steel blade or in a blender container; cover and process until well blended. Makes about 1 1/4 cups of Pesto

CINCO DE MAYO CASSEROLE

Ingredients

- 1 1/2 cups yellow cornmeal
- 1 (8 oz) container sour cream
- 1 teaspoon salt
- 2 cups shredded romaine or iceberg
- 4 cups Cold water - lettuce
- 2 tablespoons butter/margarine
- 1 cup shredded sharp cheddar
- 1 cup shredded sharp cheddar - cheese
- 2 Plum tomatoes - diced
- 5 cups Double-header chili
- 2 Green onions – sliced heated
- 1/2 Ripe avocado - diced

TOPPINGS:

- 1/2 cup Pitted sliced ripe olives

Directions

This dish is a hearty chili turned into a party dish by adding a cornmeal layer and a garnish of cut-up veggies.

Prep time: 30 minutes plus cooling Cooking time: 25 minutes Cornmeal layer: whisk cornmeal, salt, and water together in a large saucepan. Bring to boil over medium-high heat, whisking constantly. Cook until thickened, 1-2 minutes. Remove from heat and stir in butter and cheese until melted.

Immediately pour cornmeal mixture into shallow 3-quart casserole. Cool until firm, 30 minutes. (Can be made ahead. Cover and refrigerate chili and cornmeal layers separately. Assemble casserole, cover, and bake in preheated 375~ oven 1 hour or until heated through.) Preheat oven to 375~. Spread top of casserole with chili. Cover and bake 25 minutes or until heated through. Garnish with toppings.

Makes 8 servings.

CITRUS BARBECUE SAUCE

Ingredients

- 1 each Onion; Large - Finely Chopped
- 1 tablespoon Ground Red Chiles
- 1/4 teaspoon Ground Red Pepper
- 1 each Ancho Chile*
- 1 tablespoon Vegetable Oil
- 1 cup Orange Juice
- 1/2 cup Lime Juice

- 2 tablespoons Sugar
- 2 tablespoons Lemon Juice
- 1 tablespoon Fresh Cilantro - Snipped
- 1 teaspoon salt

* Ancho chile should be seeded and finely chopped.

Directions

Cook onion, ground red chiles, red pepper, and ancho chile in oil, frequently stirring, until onion is tender, about 5 minutes. Stir in the remaining ingredients. Heat to boiling, reduce heat to low. Simmer uncovered, about 10 minutes, stirring occasionally. Makes about 2 1/3 cups of sauce.

CORN AND WALNUT DIP

Ingredients

- 16 ounces Cream Cheese; Softened
- 1/4 cup Vegetable Oil
- 1/4 cup Lime Juice
- 1 tablespoon Red Chiles - Ground
- 1 tablespoon Cumin - Ground
- 1/2 teaspoon salt
- Pepper to tasty
- 8 3/4 ounces Corn; Whole Kernel - Drained
- 1 cup Walnuts - Chopped
- 1/4 cup Onion; Chopped - 1 small

Directions

Beat all ingredients except corn, walnuts, and onion in a large bowl, with an electric mixer on medium speed, until smooth. Stir in corn, walnuts, and onion.

Serve with tortilla chips. Makes 4 cups of dip.

CORN SALSA

Ingredients

- 16 ounces Corn; Canned - Drained
- 4 ounces Green Chilies; Canned - Drain
- 1 each Jalapeno Chile*
- 1/4 cup Green Bell Pepper - Chopped
- 1/4 cup Green Onions w/tops - Sliced
- 2 tablespoons White Wine Vinegar
- 1 tablespoon Vegetable Oil
- 1/4 teaspoon salt

* Jalapeno chile should be seeded and finely chopped.

Directions

Mix all ingredients. Cover and refrigerate until chilled, about 1 hour. Makes about 2 1/3 cups of Salsa.

CORN TORTILLAS

Ingredients

- 2 cups masa harina
- 1 1/3 cups warm water

Directions

Stir masa harina and water together until dough holds together in a ball. Turn onto a working surface that has been dusted with masa harina. Knead quickly into a smooth ball. Divide dough into twelve pieces. Roll one piece into a ball. Place between two sheets of wax paper and flatten slightly. Press tortillas (still in wax paper) in a tortilla press until the tortilla measures about 6 inches in diameter. Repeat with remaining pieces of dough, stacking tortillas, still sandwiched in wax paper, under a damp tea towel until ready for use.

When you're ready to cook the tortillas, preheat a seasoned cast iron griddle over medium-high heat. Remove wax paper from the tortilla and heat on the griddle, frequently turning until it looks dry and has a golden color, about 1 to 2 minutes. Repeat with remaining tortillas.

CORN-SALSA PITA SANDWICHES

Ingredients

SANDWICHES:

- 4 ears of corn
- 1 1/2 cups shredded red cabbage
- 1 green bell pepper - chopped
- 1 tomato - chopped
- 6 bacon slices - cooked
- 6 pitas
- 1 1/2 cups cheddar cheese - shredded

SALSA:

- 1 cup sour cream
- 3 tablespoons lime juice
- 2 tablespoons chopped onions
- 1 garlic clove - minced
- 1 teaspoon chili powder
- 1 teaspoon ground cumin
- 1/2 teaspoon sugar
- 1/4 teaspoon salt

- 1/4 teaspoon cayenne pepper

* Only fresh corn will make this sandwich taste its very best but use well-drained canned corn if necessary.

Directions

SALSA: Mix all the salsa ingredients well and chill.

SANDWICHES:

Remove husks from corn, remove corn silk and snap off ends of stalks. Have a pot of salted water boiling rapidly. Drop-in corn ears, cover, and cook for 5-7 minutes.

Remove corn from water, drain, and cut corn from the cob.

Combine finely shredded cabbage, green pepper, tomato, and cooked crumbled bacon in a large bowl. Stir in 3/4 cup of the salsa mix, blending well.

Cover and chill mixture. When ready to serve, fill pita bread with corn mixture, top with remaining salsa, and shredded cheese.

COWBOY CAVIAR

Ingredients

- 15 ounces Black Beans - Rinse & Drain*
- 4 ounces Ripe Olives - Chop & Drained*
- 1/4 cup Onion; Finely Chopped
- 1 each Clove Garlic - Finely Chopped
- 2 tablespoons Vegetable Oil
- 2 tablespoons Lime Juice
- 1/4 teaspoon salt

- 1/4 teaspoon Red Pepper - Crushed
- 1/4 teaspoon Cumin - Ground
- 1/8 teaspoon Pepper
- 8 ounces Cream Cheese; Softened
- 2 each egg; Large Hard-Cooked**
- 1 each Green Onion w/Top - Sliced

* 1 can of each black bean and ripe olives. Drain and rinse the beans; drain the chopped ripe olives.
** Eggs should be peeled and chopped.

Directions

Mix all ingredients except cream cheese, eggs, and green onion. Cover and refrigerate for at least 2 hours. Spread cream cheese on the serving plate. Spoon bean mixture evenly over cream cheese.

Arrange eggs on bean mixture in a ring around the edge of the plate; sprinkle with green onion.

CROCKPOT CHILE STEW

Ingredients

- 1 whole chicken - cut up
- 4 cups Water
- 10 Oz can cream of mushroom
- Or cream of chicken soup
- 12 Corn tortillas
- 1 teaspoon Garlic salt
- 1 package chicken gravy mix
- 1/2 cup Chopped green chile

Directions

Cook chicken in the crockpot with water to cover, about 4 hours. Add remaining ingredients in the last half hour of cooking. Allow boiling until tortillas are tender. Serve over rice. Makes 5 - 6 servings.

CUCUMBER SALSA

Ingredients

- 1 cup Dairy Sour Cream
- 1 cup Yogurt - Plain
- 1/4 cup Parsley - Snipped
- 1/4 cup Cilantro; Fresh - Snipped
- 1 teaspoon Cumin - Ground
- 1/2 teaspoon salt
- 2 each Cucumber - Medium *

* Cucumbers should be pared, seeded, and coarsely shredded.

Directions

Mix all ingredients. Cover and refrigerate until chilled, about 2 hours. Makes about 3 cups of salsa.

DELUXE NACHOS

Ingredients

REFRIED BEANS

- 2 cups dry pinto beans
- 1 large Onion
- 1 Ham hock - Water
- 1/2 cup Lard
- Salt

NACHOS

- 12 Corn tortillas
- Lard for deep frying
- Salt
- 1 cup shredded Jack cheese
- 1 cup shredded cheddar cheese
- 2 Jalapeno chiles (or more) - finely chopped
- 1 cup finely diced tomatoes
- 1 cup finely chopped cilantro

Directions

Place beans, whole onion, and ham hock in a saucepan. Add water to the cover.

Bring to boil, cover and simmer 1 1/2 hours, or until beans are tender.

Remove onion and ham hock. Drain beans. Heat lard until very hot. Add to beans and mash with a potato masher. Season to taste with salt. Set aside. To make nachos, cut tortillas in quarters and fry in deep hot lard until crisp. Drain and season lightly with salt. Arrange tortillas in a single layer on a large ovenproof platter. Sprinkle half each of Jack and cheddar cheeses over tortilla chips.

Sprinkle chiles over cheeses. Top with dollops of refried beans and gently spread over the mixture. (Reserve any extra beans for another use.) Sprinkle with half of the remaining cheeses. Top with tomatoes and cilantro, then with remaining cheeses. Bake at 375F until cheeses are melted and bubbly, about 15 minutes. Serve at once.

DIABLO JALAPENO JELLY

Ingredients

- 1 green bell pepper
- 5 jalapeno peppers
- 3 cups sugar
- 3/4 cup cider vinegar
- 3 ounces pectin
- 2 drops green food coloring

Directions

Sterilize jelly jars and lids according to the manufacturer's instructions.

Remove seeds from green pepper and chilies (Be very careful with chiles - don't touch your eyes.) Fit the steel knife blade into the bowl. Chop green pepper into 1/4-inch pieces. Measure 1/2 cup. Reserve rest for another purpose. Chop jalapenos into 1/4-inch pieces. Measure 1/4 cup for jelly.

Place the 1/2 cup green pepper and 1/4 cup jalapenos, sugar, and vinegar in a large saucepan. Bring to a boil. Continue to boil for 1 minute. Remove from heat; let cool for 5 minutes. Stir in pectin and food coloring.

Strain mixture through a fine strainer to remove pieces of peppers. Pour the strained liquid into sterilized jars. Cover tightly and store in a cool place for up to 6 months.

Makes 2 cups.

Serving Ideas: Serve with scrambled eggs and meats.

EASY NACHOS

Ingredients

- 8 ounces Tortilla chips
- 8 ounces Velveeta Shredded Process - Cheese food
- 8 ounces Pace Thick & Chunky Salsa

OPTIONAL GARNISHES

- Ripe olives - sliced
- Guacamole

- Jalapeno peppers - sliced
- Sour cream

Directions

Place tortilla chips on a baking sheet; sprinkle with cheese food. Bake at 350~ until cheese food melts, 3-4 minutes. Pour Pace Thick & Chunky Salsa over chips.

Garnish as desired.

MICROWAVE OVEN DIRECTIONS: Microwave a 9" plateful of cheese food-topped chips at HIGH 1 minute or until cheese food melts.

EGG TACOS

Ingredients

- 1/2 medium onion
- 1 jalapeno pepper - seeded
- 1/2 sweet red pepper - seeded
- 5 tablespoons olive oil
- 6 eggs - separated
- 2 tablespoons milk
- 1 tablespoon chili powder
- 4 flour tortillas
- 1 large tomato - chopped

- 4 ounces Monterey jack cheese - shredded
- Picante sauce - to taste
- salt and pepper

Directions

Chop onions and peppers and saute in two tablespoons olive oil until limp.

Beat egg yolks with milk, chili powder, and salt and pepper to taste.

Stir in cooked onions and peppers.

Beat egg whites separately until stiff. Fold into egg yolk mixture. Heat remaining olive oil in a large, oven-safe skillet.

Spread egg mixture in skillet and cook until eggs are set on bottom. Place pan under the broiler until the top is brown. Heat tortillas.

To serve, divide the egg mixture into four parts. Place a piece of egg in the center of the tortilla. Top with cheese, tomato, and Picante sauce to taste. Fold tortilla over the egg.

EGGS MOTUL STYLE

Ingredients

- 1 1/2 cups Black Beans; Dry - 8 oz
- 3 cups Water
- 1/4 cup Onion; Chopped
- 1 each Clove Garlic - Minced
- 1 teaspoon salt
- 8 ounces Tomatoes; Finely Chopped
- 2 tablespoons Onion - Finely Chopped

- 1/2 teaspoon salt
- 1/8 teaspoon Cayenne Pepper
- Vegetable Oil
- 10 ounces Peas; Frozen
- 1 1/2 cups Ham - Chopped
- 8 each Corn Tortillas - 8" Diameter
- 8 each Egg - Large
- 2 ounces Monterey Jack Cheese*

* There should be about 1/2 cup of the shredded cheese.

Directions

In a large saucepan, soak the beans overnight in the water. (Or bring to boiling, simmer for 2 minutes, cover and let stand for 1 hour.) Do not drain. Add 1/4 cup of onion, garlic, and 1 tsp of salt. Then cook for another 2 hours or until very tender.

Combine the UNDRAINED tomatoes, the 2 tbs of chopped onion, 1/2 tsp of salt, and cayenne. Set aside. Heat the 2 tbs of vegetable oil in a large, heavy skillet. Add the beans with the liquid, mash the beans in the skillet.

Cook, uncovered, over medium heat 3 to 5 minutes or until very thick. Cook peas according to the directions on the package and drain. Toss with the ham; cover and keep warm.

Heat 1/4 inch of vegetable oil in another heavy skillet. Fry tortillas 20 to 40 seconds per side or until crisp and golden. Drain on paper toweling.

Spread about 1/3 cup of the bean mixture on each tortilla and keep them warm in a 300-degree F oven.

In the same oil, fry the eggs until they are set. Season with salt and pepper. Place an egg on the top of each bean-covered tortilla. Sprinkle each with about 1/2 cup of the ham mixture. Spoon some of the tomato sauce on top and sprinkle with the cheese. Serve hot

Lightning Source UK Ltd.
Milton Keynes UK
UKHW020814110621
385331UK00004B/55